EXOTIC DUCK DECOYS
FOR THE WOODCARVER
With Full-Size Templates

DOVER PUBLICATIONS, INC., NEW YORK

The authors wish to thank Arlene Saunders and John Steed
for use of technical data from their libraries.

Original carvings of the birds found in this book (as well as other carvings) may be obtained by writing directly to the authors:

Mr. Anthony Hillman
"Hillman's Baycraft"
1818 Shore Road—Seaville
Ocean View P.O., New Jersey 08230

Mr. Harry V. Shourds
"The Ducks Nest"
2025 South Shore Road—Seaville
Ocean View P.O., New Jersey 08230

Copyright © 1984 by Harry V. Shourds and Anthony Hillman.
All rights reserved under Pan American and International Copyright Conventions.

Published in Canada by General Publishing Company, Ltd., 30 Lesmill Road, Don Mills, Toronto, Ontario.

Published in the United Kingdom by Constable and Company, Ltd., 10 Orange Street, London WC2H 7EG.

Exotic Duck Decoys for the Woodcarver: With Full-Size Templates is a new work, first published in 1984 by Dover Publications, Inc.

These patterns and drawings are not to be used for printed reproduction without permission.

Manufactured in the United States of America
Dover Publications, Inc., 31 East 2nd Street, Mineola, N.Y. 11501

Library of Congress Cataloging in Publication Data

Shourds, Harry V.
Exotic duck decoys for the woodcarver, with full-size templates.

Bibliography: p.
1. Wood-carving. 2. Decoys (Hunting) I. Hillman, Anthony. II. Title.
TT199.7.S56 1984   745.593   83-20578
ISBN 0-486-24667-1

HOW TO USE THIS BOOK

Over many generations, the people of the South Jersey region have developed a distinctive style of carving wooden duck decoys. The hollow, two-piece body construction of these decoys makes them particularly attractive, not only for aesthetic, but for practical reasons. A hunter will find that these decoys will float better than solid ones, riding the water more naturally and less likely to become waterlogged. The light weight of the hollow body makes it easier for a collector to display a large number of these decoys on a shelf or wall mounting. The patterns in this book follow the essential characteristics of the South Jersey decoy. Most of the decoys in this book are of exotic and less common species of ducks.

Remove the staples and spread the pages out flat. You can cut out the patterns and use them directly as templates, but we recommend that you give them permanence by gluing them to 3/16" mahogany exterior plywood. Mahogany is recommended because even pieces as thin as these will be durable. Carefully recut the patterns. Varnish will seal the edges. Mounting the patterns in this manner will preserve them for making duplicates, for which we have supplied on some patterns alternative heads, either of the female, or else for the preening position.

Each pattern includes the profile and top view of the body. On some of the larger bird patterns we have used half-widths for the top views. Cut this type of pattern out, trace it, and then flip it over and retrace it for a complete top-view pattern. For each of the 16 decoys we specify the minimum-size pieces of dressed wood that you will need.

Each main head pattern has been drawn connected to the body to give a sense of how the head and body will look together. They are to be separated for use as templates and are to be carved on separate pieces of wood.

On the head template, drill a hole in the eye big enough for marking eye position. Generally, all ducks have similar structure when viewed from the front, the most important differences being in the bills. Therefore, for the shoveler we have provided an illustration of the top view of the head.

The profile patterns can be left with the head and body connected for use in designing carved or painted plaques, needlepoint, or whatever else you can think of.

HOW TO MAKE AN EXOTIC DUCK DECOY BY THE TRADITIONAL SOUTH JERSEY METHOD

The Body

Let's make a Gadwall. For the body use two pieces of dressed wood 6" wide, one piece being 2¼" thick and 14" long, the other piece 2" thick and 12½" long. Tape the two pieces of wood together with masking tape. Position the pattern so that the center line falls right along the line made where the two pieces of wood are joined. Mark out the profile pattern as shown in Fig. 1.

Fig. 1.

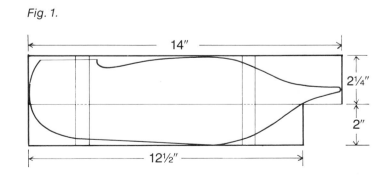

Cut this out on a band saw, being careful to cut along the *outside* of the thick black line. Now separate the pieces, and using the top-view pattern mark each piece on the surfaces which were joined, and then bandsaw the top and bottom halves. The dashed line on the top-view pattern indicates the shape of the bottom half. Do not cut too close to the thick black lines—leave a little extra for the final shaping. Shape top and bottom halves individually, fitting the two together periodically to insure a nice rounded shape. Using a hatchet or a drawknife, cut away excess wood to get the general shape (Fig. 2). A spokeshave is used to further round and smooth the body. Leave extra surface for the neck joint.

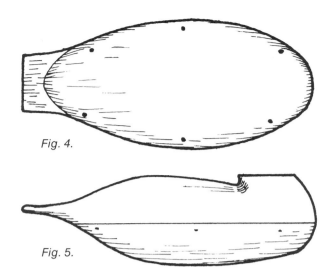
Fig. 4.

Fig. 5.

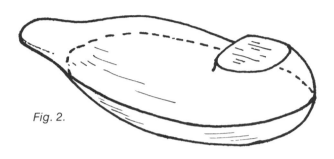
Fig. 2.

nailing the bottom to the top (Fig. 4). Further smooth and fair the body with a spokeshave or rasp (Fig. 5).

The Head

There are several ways to hollow out a decoy body. One way is to use a 1″ gouge (about a 9 sweep) and a mallet. Score the wood about ¾″ from the edge to prevent splitting to the outside edge. Hollow the top section to within ½″. Leave more wood in the middle of the bottom body section so you can weight it (Fig. 3a and Fig. 3b). Other methods include drilling with hand drills or a drill press with Forstner bits if available. When using a drill press be sure to secure the half being drilled and to pay attention to the depth of the cut.

Now assemble the two halves, using a good waterproof glue, and toenail using 3DD galvanized finishing nails,

The head of your decoy will demand more time and effort than the body. Generally, what you want to achieve in your carving, especially of the head, is symmetry of form. In other words, the eyes should be opposite each other! Also, both cheeks should be equally puffy, and the neck and top of the head should have the same graceful curves on either side. Many superdetailed decorative carvings are spoiled simply because of unevenness in the basic carving.

Using a piece of pine or other suitable wood 2″ thick, 4″ high and 5½″ long, lay the head profile pattern so that the grain of the wood runs *with the bill*. Make sure the base of the neck is even with the bottom edge of the wood. Cut out on a band saw. After sawing out the head shape, measure the half-thickness of your stock. With a pencil, mark down the middle of the entire head block on all sawn surfaces. *Never cut this line away!* It is the cross-section of the head and should be there when you finish-sand your carving.

At this point you may want to drill guide holes for the eyes, while the sides of the head are flat. Use a drill press if available (Fig. 6).

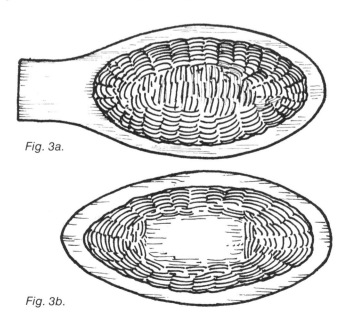
Fig. 3a.

Fig. 3b.

Fig. 6.

Introduction continues after templates.

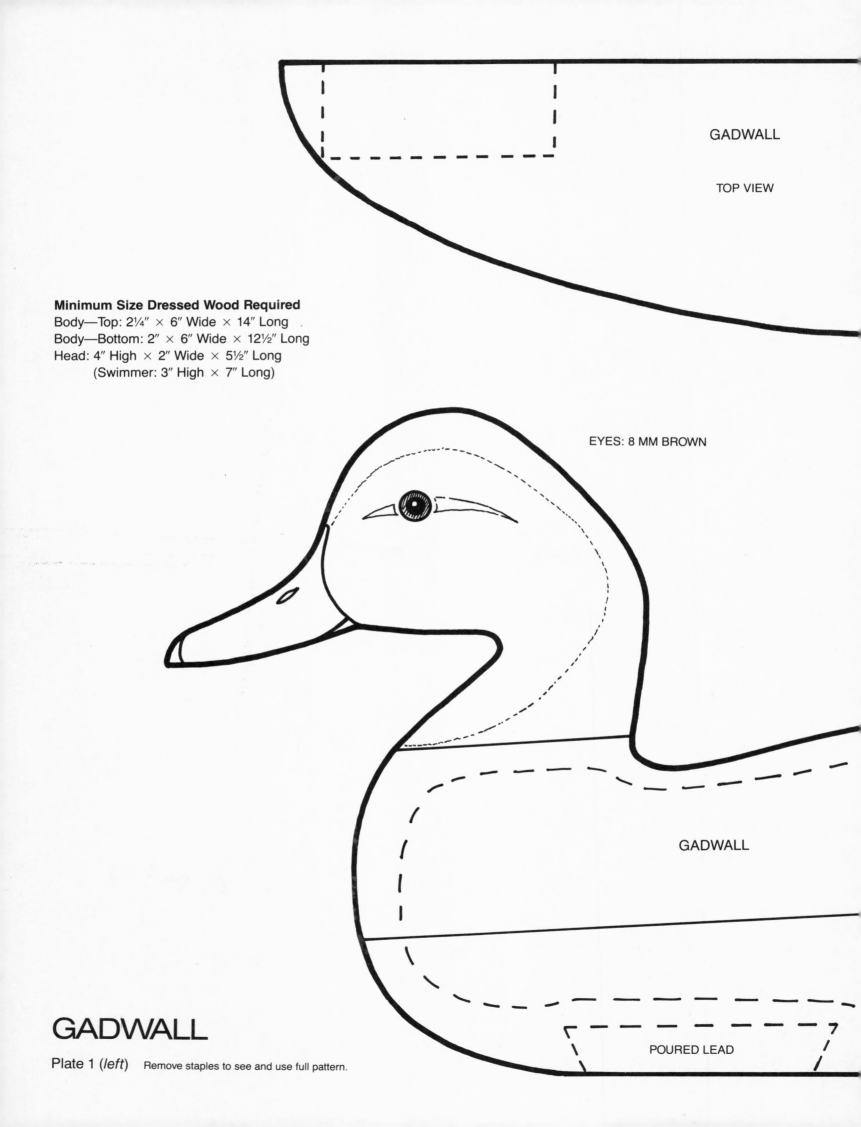

GADWALL

TOP VIEW

Minimum Size Dressed Wood Required
Body—Top: 2¼″ × 6″ Wide × 14″ Long
Body—Bottom: 2″ × 6″ Wide × 12½″ Long
Head: 4″ High × 2″ Wide × 5½″ Long
        (Swimmer: 3″ High × 7″ Long)

EYES: 8 MM BROWN

GADWALL

POURED LEAD

GADWALL

Plate 1 (*left*)   Remove staples to see and use full pattern.

RING-NECKED DUCK

TOP VIEW

Minimum Size Dressed Wood Required
Body—Top: 2″ × 6″ Wide × 11″ Long
Body—Bottom: 1½″ × 6″ Wide × 10″ Long
Head: 3½″ High × 2″ Wide × 4½″ Long
    (Female: 2¾″ High)

EYES: 8 MM YELLOW, MALE
AMBER, FEMALE

RING-NECKED DUCK: FEMALE

HOLLOW

HOLLOW

POURED LEAD

RING-NECKED DUCK

Plate 2 (*left*)   Remove staples to see and use full pattern.

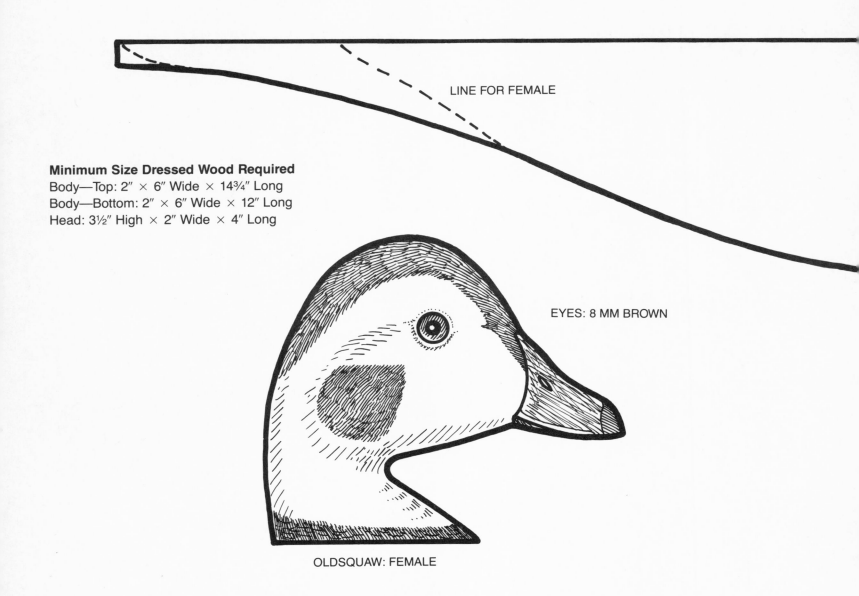

LINE FOR FEMALE

Minimum Size Dressed Wood Required
Body—Top: 2″ × 6″ Wide × 14¾″ Long
Body—Bottom: 2″ × 6″ Wide × 12″ Long
Head: 3½″ High × 2″ Wide × 4″ Long

EYES: 8 MM BROWN

OLDSQUAW: FEMALE

HOLLOW

HOLLOW

POURED LEA[D]

OLDSQUAW

Plate 3 (*left*)   Remove staples to see and use full pattern.

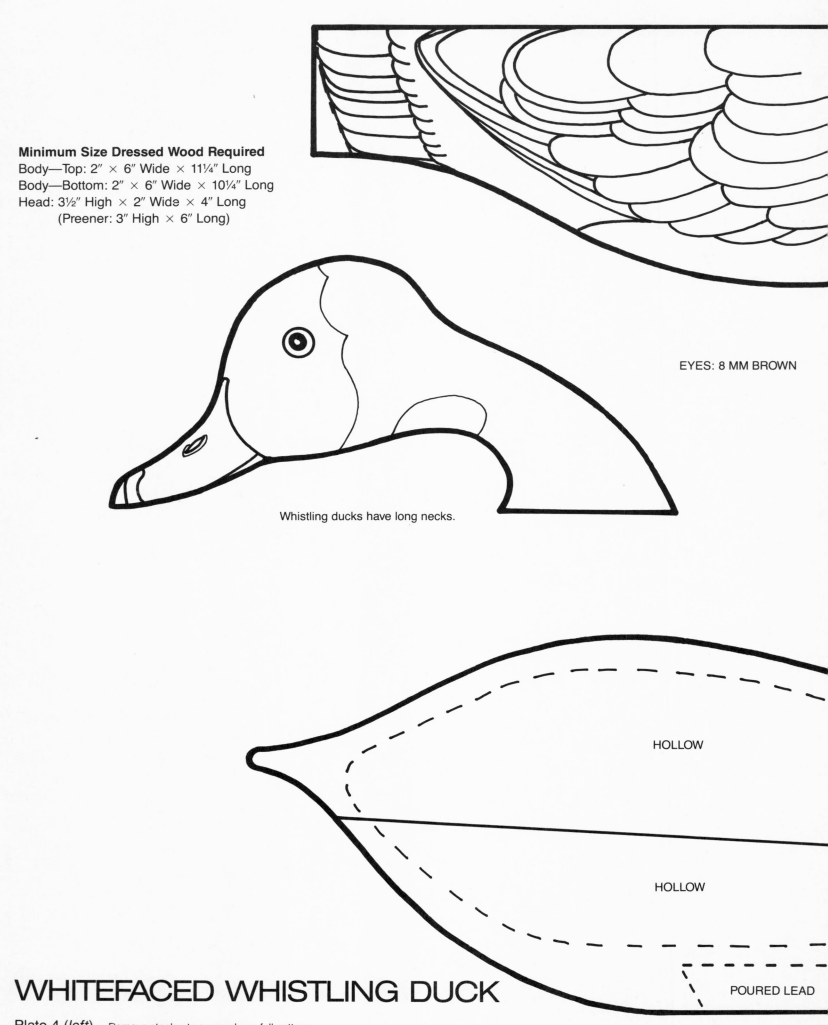

Minimum Size Dressed Wood Required
Body—Top: 2″ × 6″ Wide × 11¼″ Long
Body—Bottom: 2″ × 6″ Wide × 10¼″ Long
Head: 3½″ High × 2″ Wide × 4″ Long
    (Preener: 3″ High × 6″ Long)

EYES: 8 MM BROWN

Whistling ducks have long necks.

HOLLOW

HOLLOW

POURED LEAD

WHITEFACED WHISTLING DUCK

Plate 4 (*left*)   Remove staples to see and use full pattern.

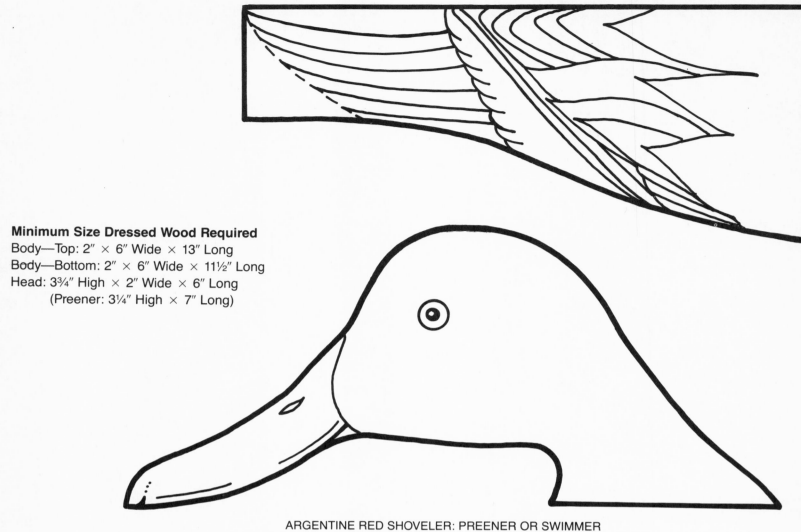

Minimum Size Dressed Wood Required
Body—Top: 2″ × 6″ Wide × 13″ Long
Body—Bottom: 2″ × 6″ Wide × 11½″ Long
Head: 3¾″ High × 2″ Wide × 6″ Long
　　　(Preener: 3¼″ High × 7″ Long)

ARGENTINE RED SHOVELER: PREENER OR SWIMMER

The male and female of this species are similar in plumage.

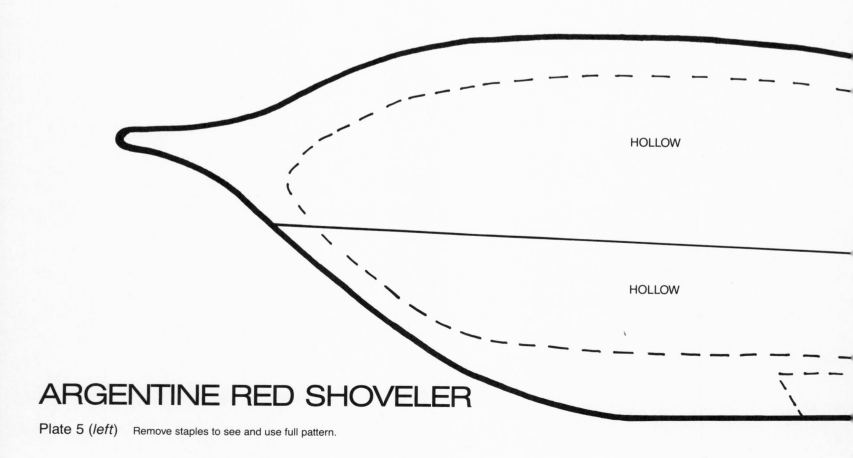

HOLLOW

HOLLOW

ARGENTINE RED SHOVELER

Plate 5 (*left*)　Remove staples to see and use full pattern.

Minimum Size Dressed Wood Required
Body—Top: 2¼″ × 5″ Wide × 10¾″ Long
Body—Bottom: 1½″ × 5″ Wide × 9½″ Long
Head: 3½″ High × 2″ Wide × 4¾″ Long
    (Preener: 3″ High × 6″ Long)

EYES: 8 MM RED, MALE
BROWN, FEMALE

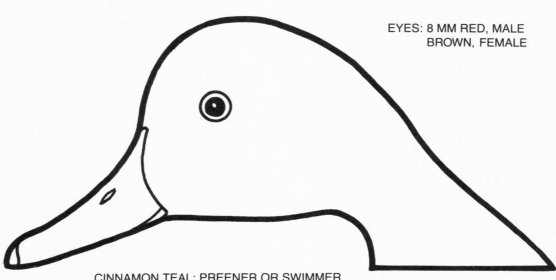

CINNAMON TEAL: PREENER OR SWIMMER

Facing backwards, this head makes a "preener."
Facing forwards it makes a "swimmer" or "feeder."

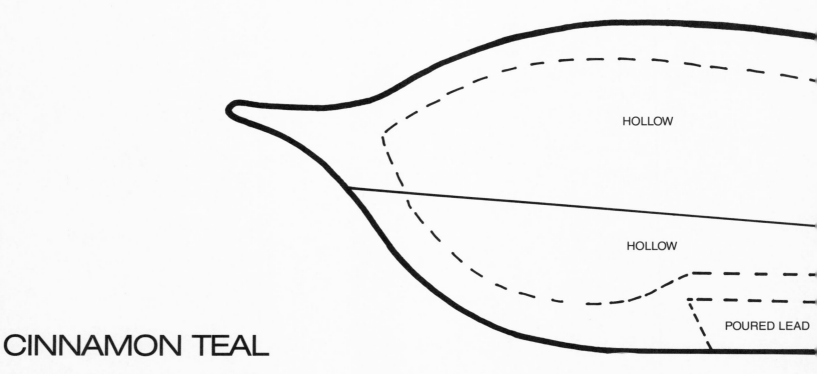

HOLLOW

HOLLOW

POURED LEAD

CINNAMON TEAL

Plate 6 (*left*)   Remove staples to see and use full pattern.

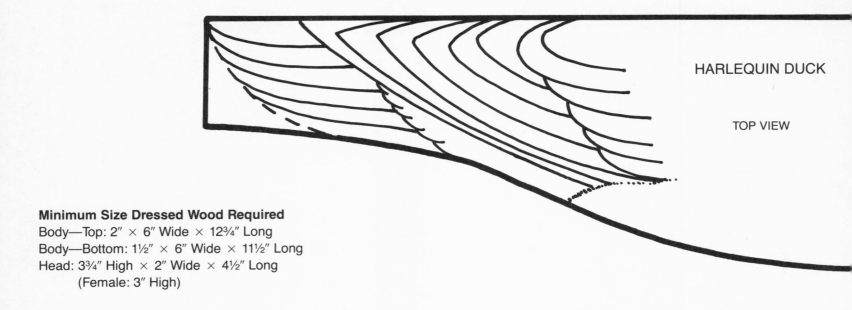

HARLEQUIN DUCK

TOP VIEW

Minimum Size Dressed Wood Required
Body—Top: 2″ × 6″ Wide × 12¾″ Long
Body—Bottom: 1½″ × 6″ Wide × 11½″ Long
Head: 3¾″ High × 2″ Wide × 4½″ Long
    (Female: 3″ High)

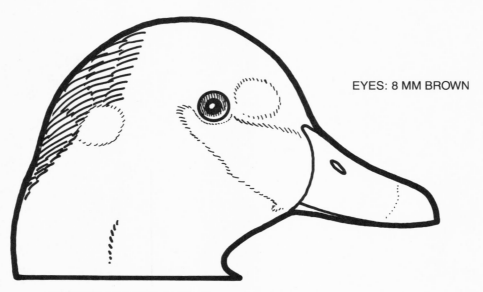

EYES: 8 MM BROWN

HARLEQUIN DUCK: FEMALE

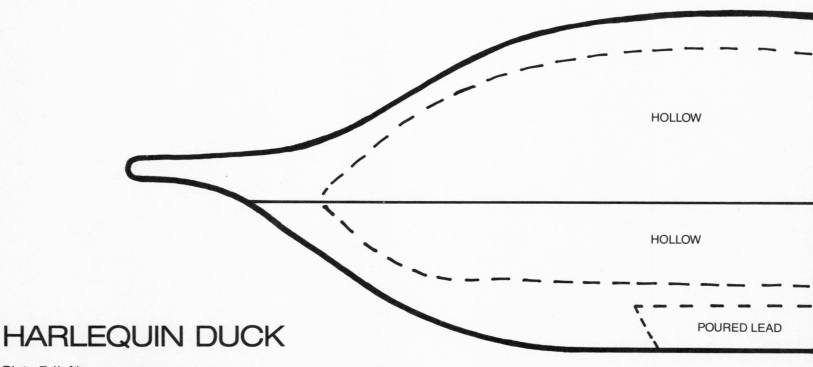

HOLLOW

HOLLOW

POURED LEAD

HARLEQUIN DUCK

Plate 7 (*left*)   Remove staples to see and use full pattern.

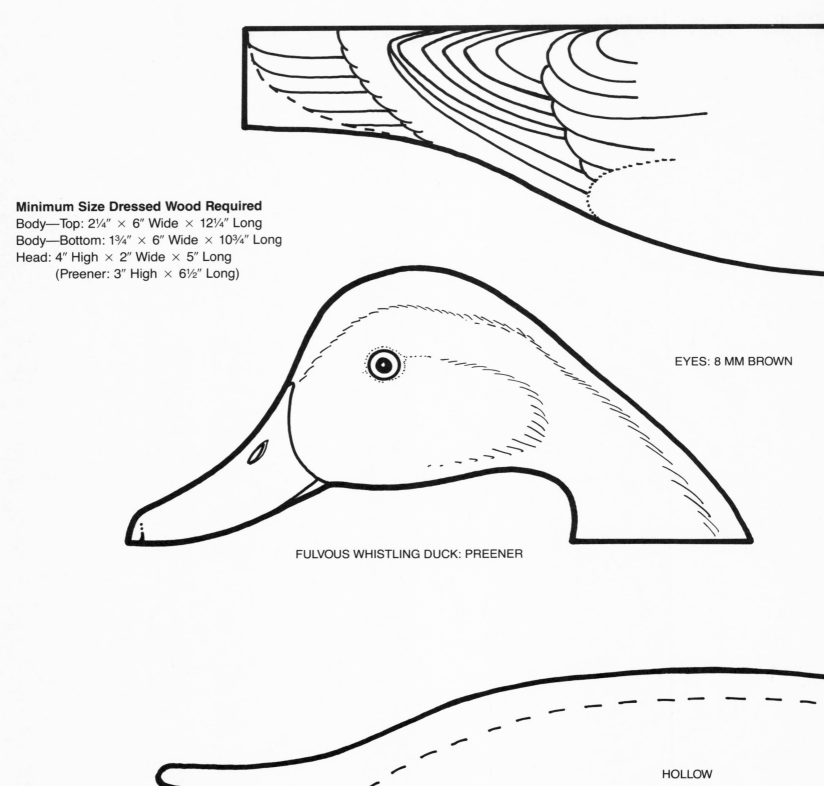

Minimum Size Dressed Wood Required
Body—Top: 2¼″ × 6″ Wide × 12¼″ Long
Body—Bottom: 1¾″ × 6″ Wide × 10¾″ Long
Head: 4″ High × 2″ Wide × 5″ Long
 (Preener: 3″ High × 6½″ Long)

EYES: 8 MM BROWN

FULVOUS WHISTLING DUCK: PREENER

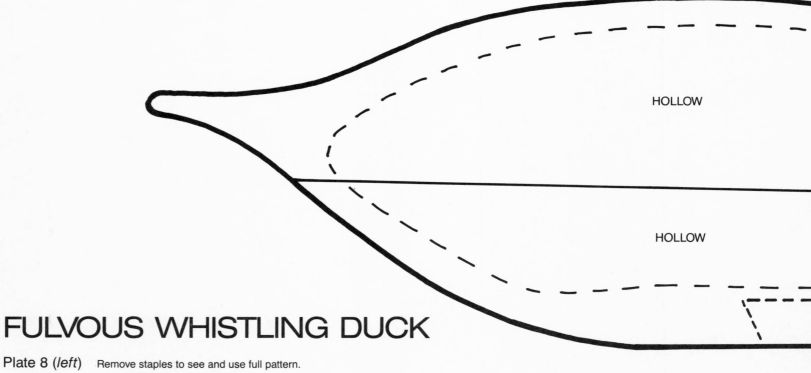

HOLLOW

HOLLOW

FULVOUS WHISTLING DUCK

Plate 8 (*left*)   Remove staples to see and use full pattern.

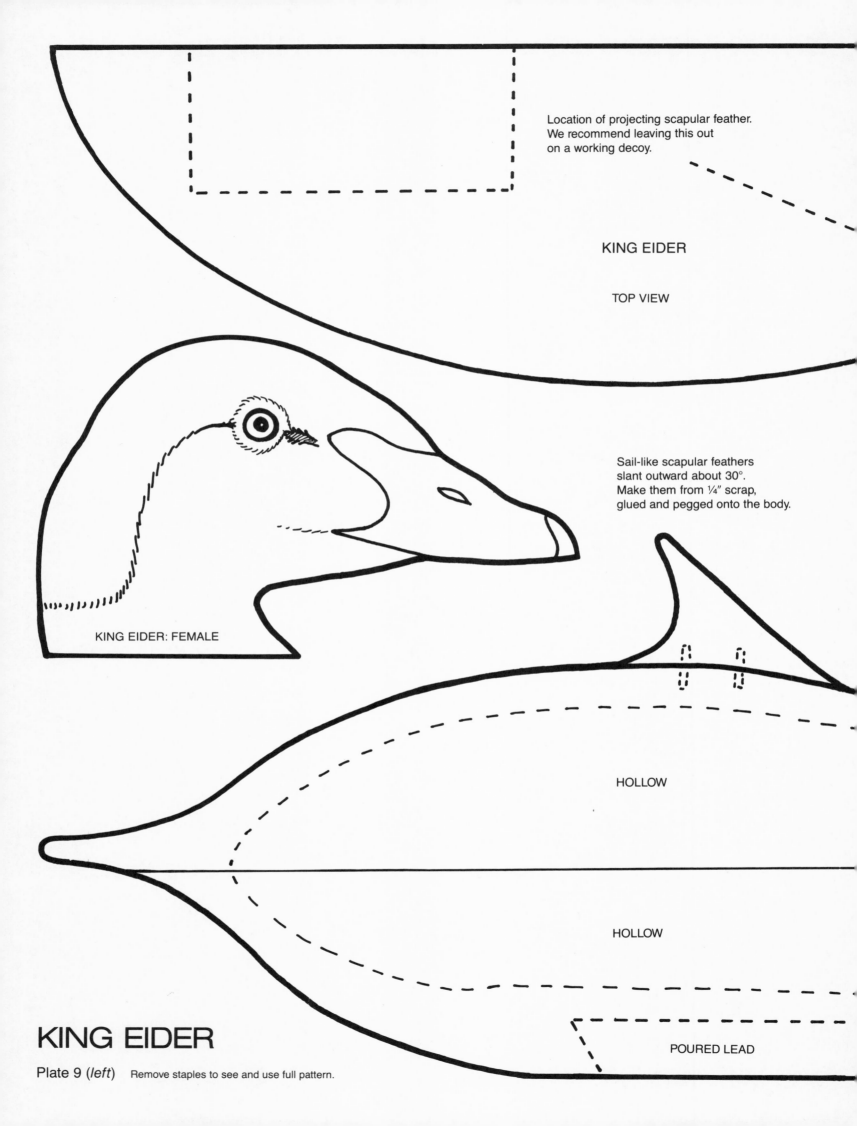

Location of projecting scapular feather.
We recommend leaving this out
on a working decoy.

KING EIDER

TOP VIEW

Sail-like scapular feathers
slant outward about 30°.
Make them from ¼" scrap,
glued and pegged onto the body.

KING EIDER: FEMALE

HOLLOW

HOLLOW

KING EIDER

Plate 9 (*left*)   Remove staples to see and use full pattern.

POURED LEAD

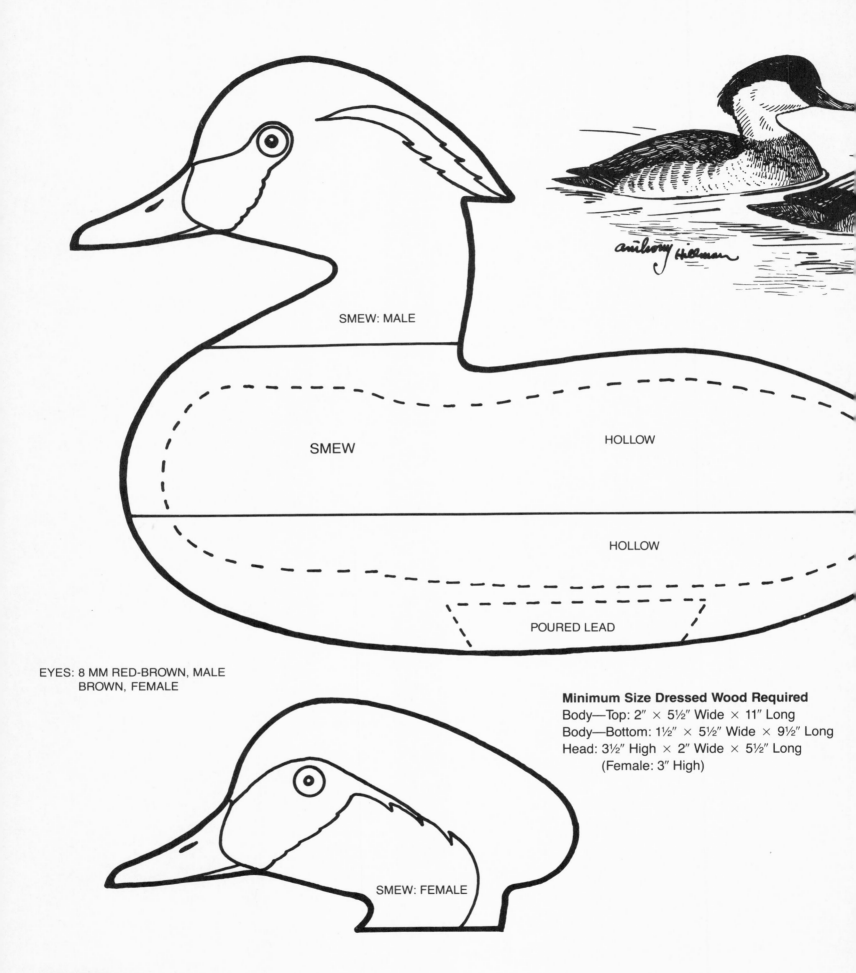

SMEW: MALE

SMEW

HOLLOW

HOLLOW

POURED LEAD

EYES: 8 MM RED-BROWN, MALE
BROWN, FEMALE

Minimum Size Dressed Wood Required
Body—Top: 2″ × 5½″ Wide × 11″ Long
Body—Bottom: 1½″ × 5½″ Wide × 9½″ Long
Head: 3½″ High × 2″ Wide × 5½″ Long
   (Female: 3″ High)

SMEW: FEMALE

SMEW

Plate 10 (*left*)   Remove staples to see and use full pattern.

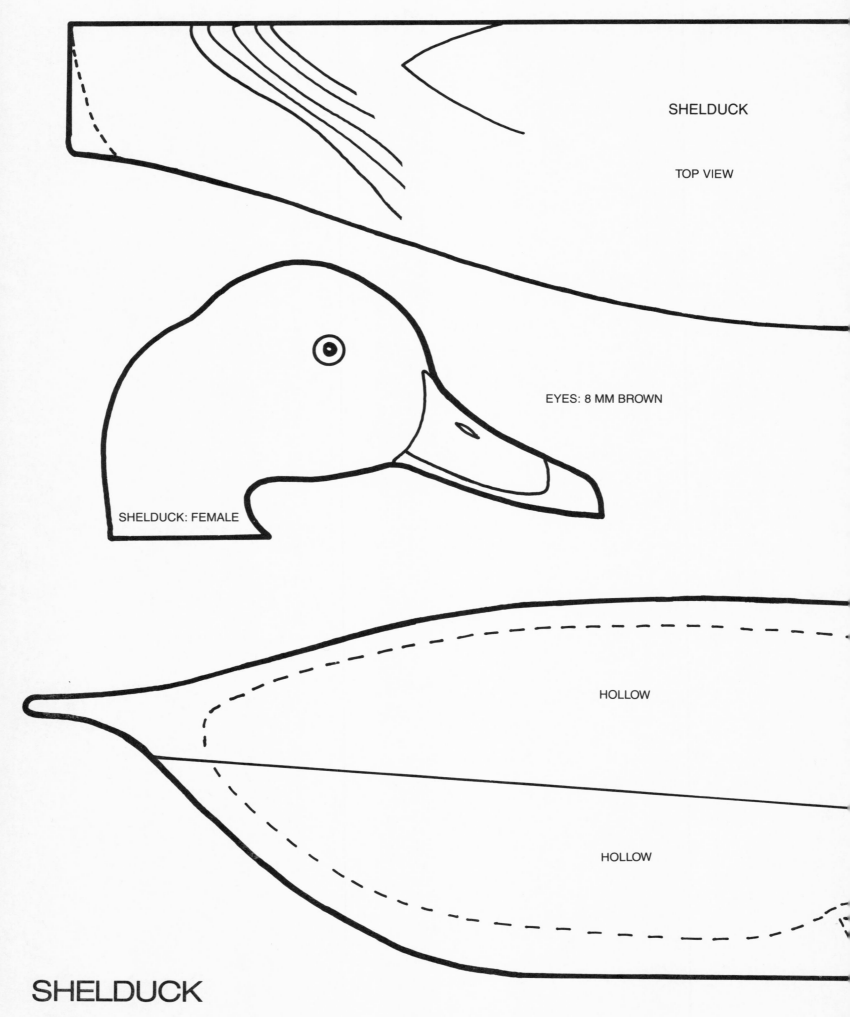

SHELDUCK

TOP VIEW

EYES: 8 MM BROWN

SHELDUCK: FEMALE

HOLLOW

HOLLOW

SHELDUCK

Plate 11 (*left*)   Remove staples to see and use full pattern.

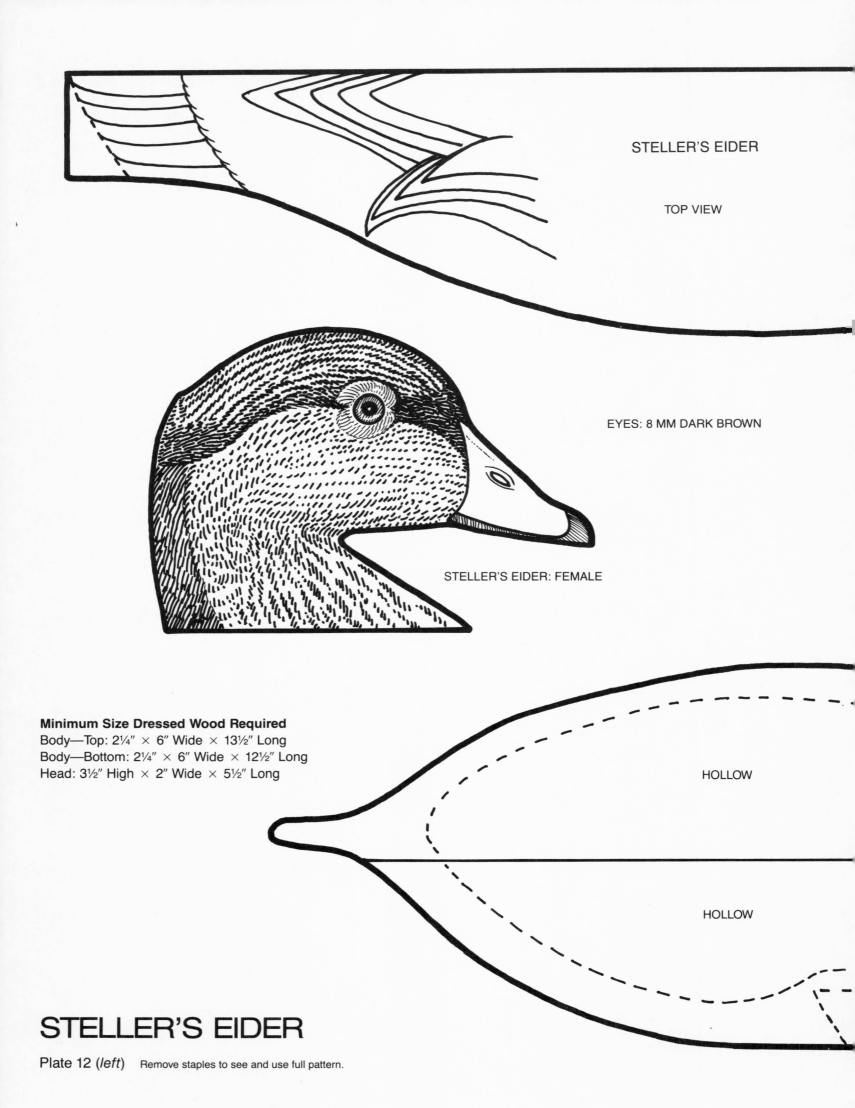

STELLER'S EIDER

TOP VIEW

EYES: 8 MM DARK BROWN

STELLER'S EIDER: FEMALE

Minimum Size Dressed Wood Required
Body—Top: 2¼″ × 6″ Wide × 13½″ Long
Body—Bottom: 2¼″ × 6″ Wide × 12½″ Long
Head: 3½″ High × 2″ Wide × 5½″ Long

HOLLOW

HOLLOW

STELLER'S EIDER

Plate 12 (*left*)   Remove staples to see and use full pattern.

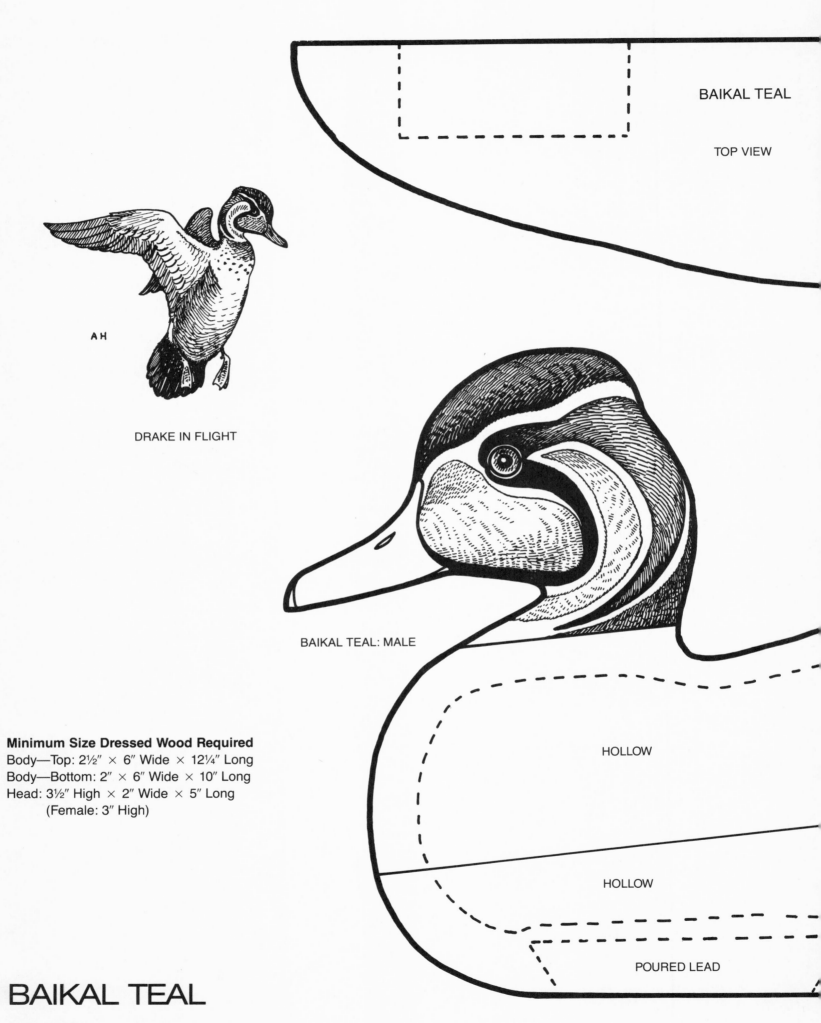

BAIKAL TEAL

TOP VIEW

DRAKE IN FLIGHT

A H

BAIKAL TEAL: MALE

Minimum Size Dressed Wood Required
Body—Top: 2½″ × 6″ Wide × 12¼″ Long
Body—Bottom: 2″ × 6″ Wide × 10″ Long
Head: 3½″ High × 2″ Wide × 5″ Long
      (Female: 3″ High)

HOLLOW

HOLLOW

POURED LEAD

BAIKAL TEAL

Plate 13 (*left*)   Remove staples to see and use full pattern.

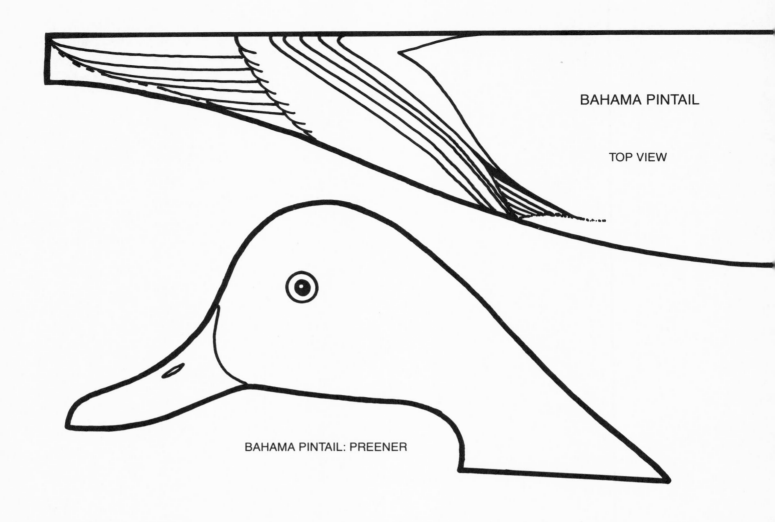

BAHAMA PINTAIL

TOP VIEW

BAHAMA PINTAIL: PREENER

The male and female of this species are similar in plumage.

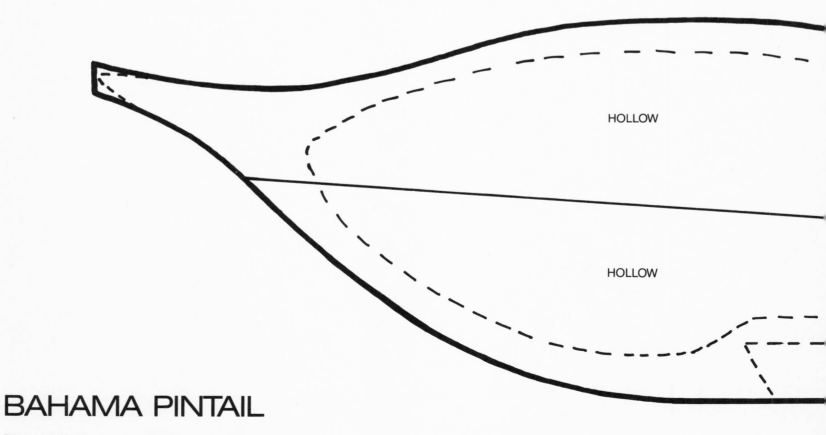

HOLLOW

HOLLOW

BAHAMA PINTAIL

Plate 14 (*left*)   Remove staples to see and use full pattern.

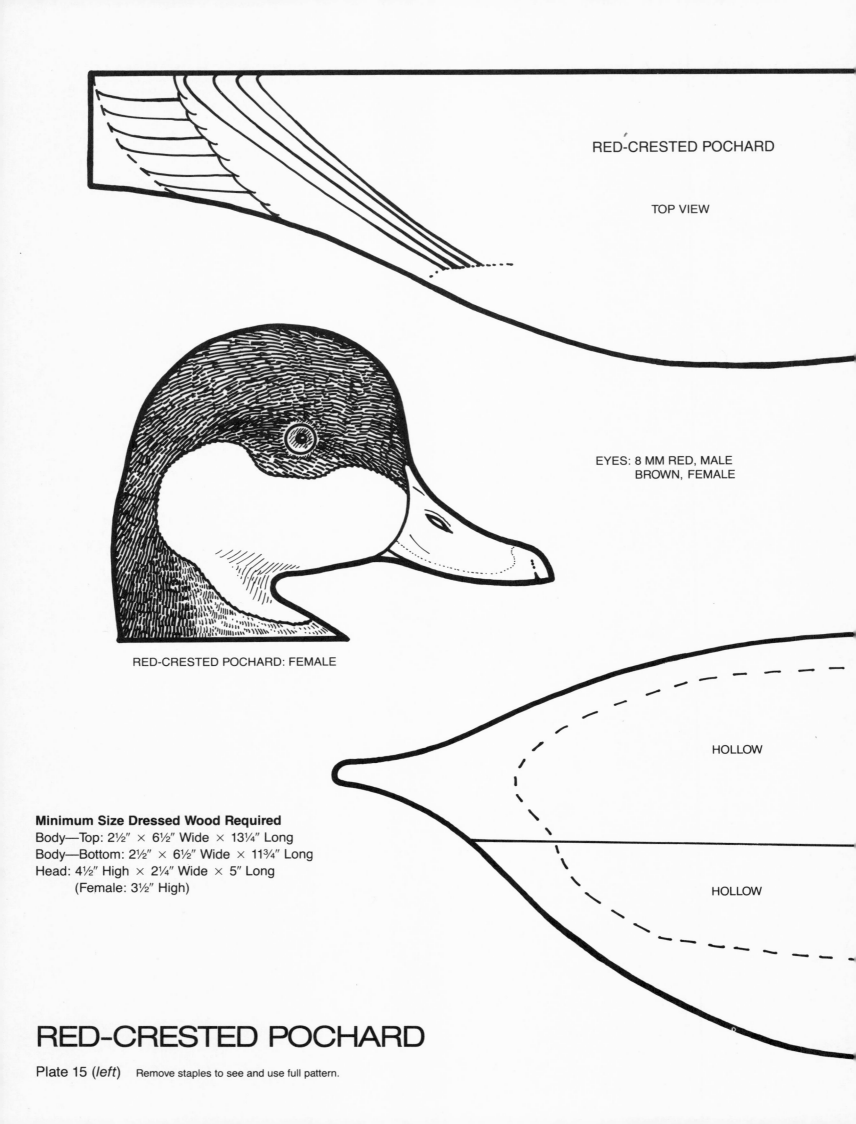

RED-CRESTED POCHARD

TOP VIEW

EYES: 8 MM RED, MALE
BROWN, FEMALE

RED-CRESTED POCHARD: FEMALE

HOLLOW

Minimum Size Dressed Wood Required
Body—Top: 2½″ × 6½″ Wide × 13¼″ Long
Body—Bottom: 2½″ × 6½″ Wide × 11¾″ Long
Head: 4½″ High × 2¼″ Wide × 5″ Long
    (Female: 3½″ High)

HOLLOW

RED-CRESTED POCHARD

Plate 15 (*left*)   Remove staples to see and use full pattern.

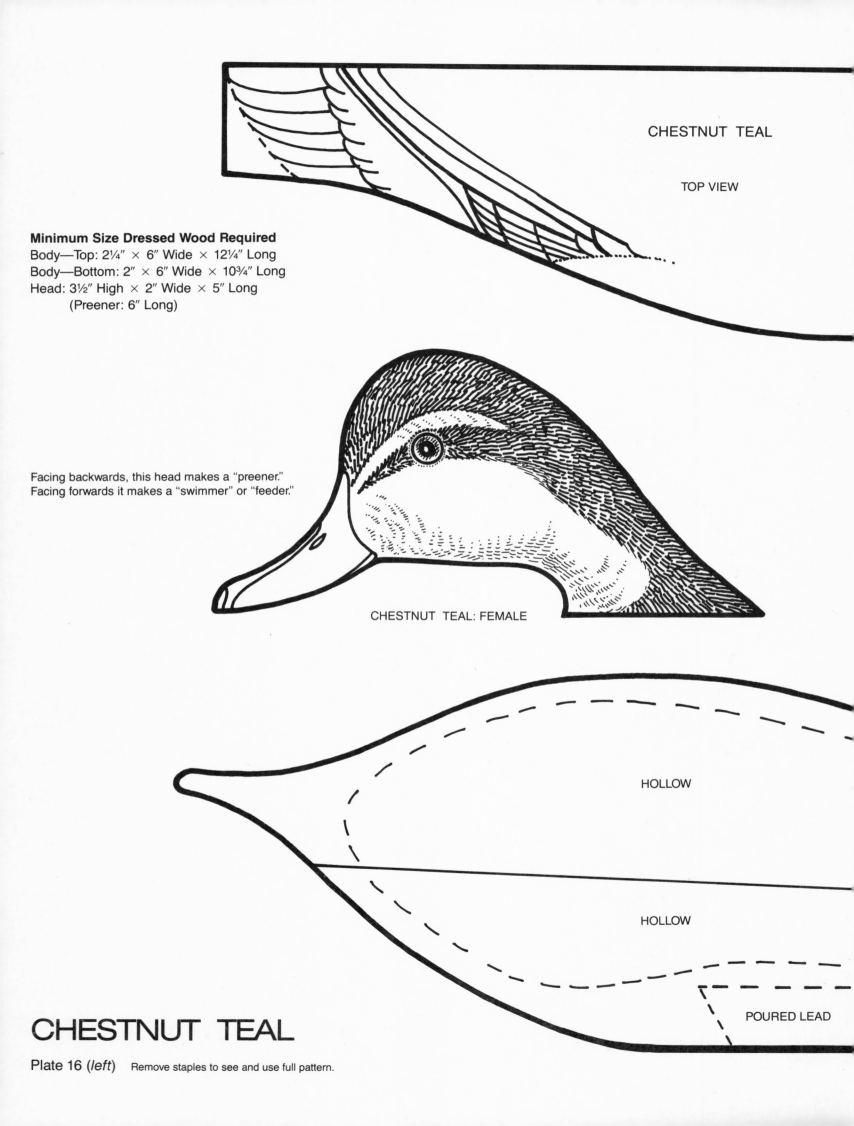

CHESTNUT TEAL

TOP VIEW

Minimum Size Dressed Wood Required
Body—Top: 2¼″ × 6″ Wide × 12¼″ Long
Body—Bottom: 2″ × 6″ Wide × 10¾″ Long
Head: 3½″ High × 2″ Wide × 5″ Long
        (Preener: 6″ Long)

Facing backwards, this head makes a "preener."
Facing forwards it makes a "swimmer" or "feeder."

CHESTNUT TEAL: FEMALE

HOLLOW

HOLLOW

POURED LEAD

CHESTNUT TEAL

Plate 16 (*left*)   Remove staples to see and use full pattern.

EYES: 8 MM RED, MALE
RED-BROWN, FEMALE

CHESTNUT TEAL: MALE

CHESTNUT TEAL

CHESTNUT TEAL

Plate 16 (*right*)   Remove staples to see and use full pattern.

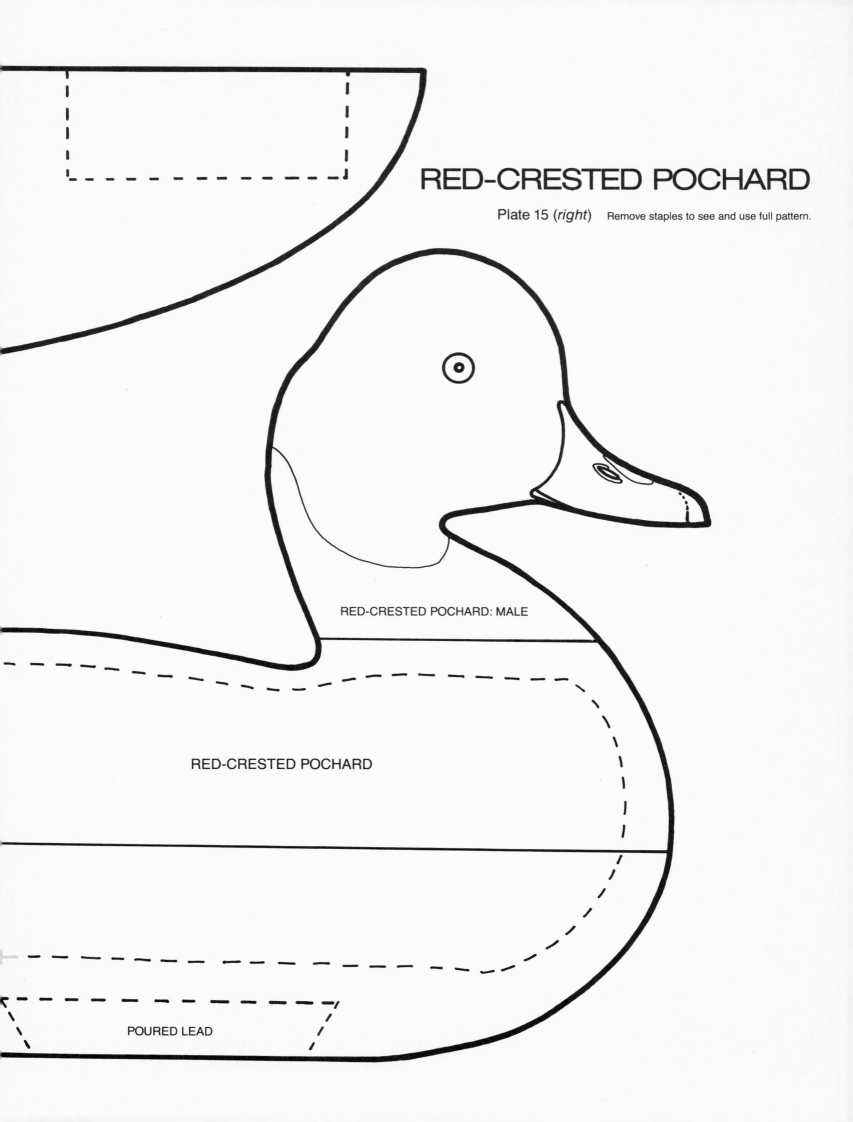

RED-CRESTED POCHARD

Plate 15 (*right*)   Remove staples to see and use full pattern.

RED-CRESTED POCHARD: MALE

RED-CRESTED POCHARD

POURED LEAD

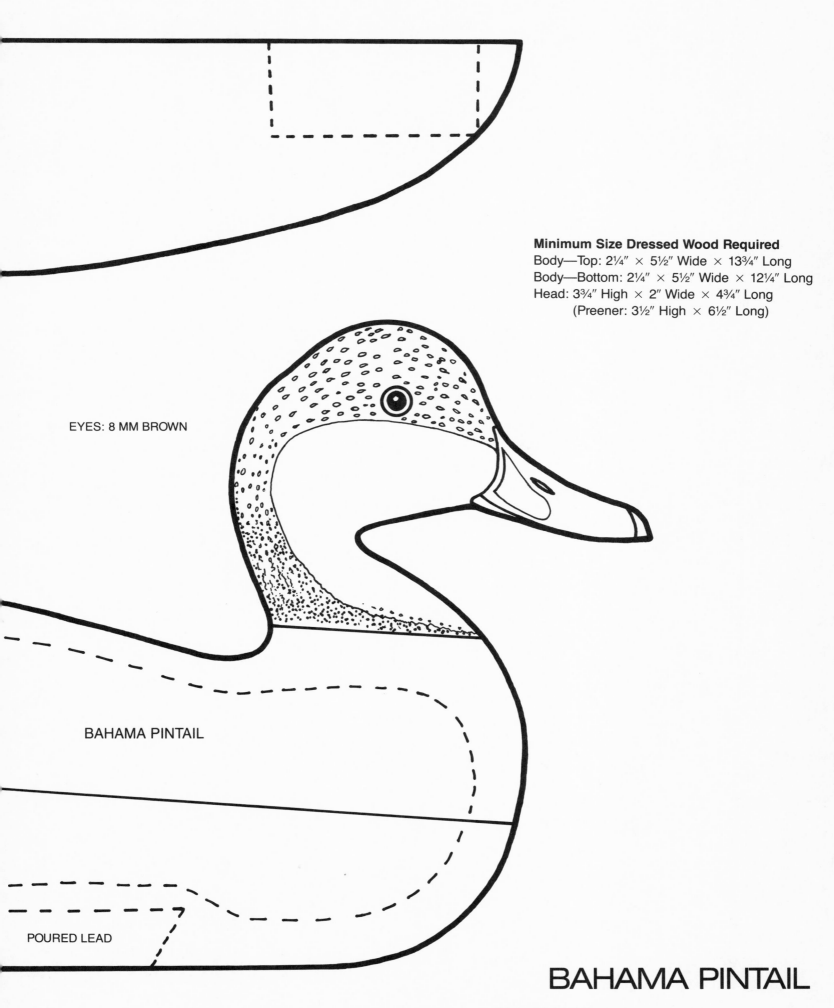

Minimum Size Dressed Wood Required
Body—Top: 2¼″ × 5½″ Wide × 13¾″ Long
Body—Bottom: 2¼″ × 5½″ Wide × 12¼″ Long
Head: 3¾″ High × 2″ Wide × 4¾″ Long
     (Preener: 3½″ High × 6½″ Long)

EYES: 8 MM BROWN

BAHAMA PINTAIL

POURED LEAD

BAHAMA PINTAIL

Plate 14 (*right*)   Remove staples to see and use full pattern.

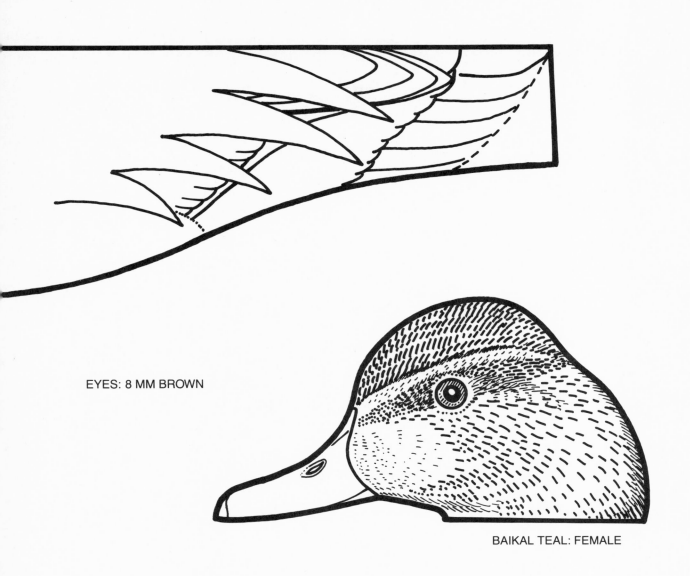

EYES: 8 MM BROWN

BAIKAL TEAL: FEMALE

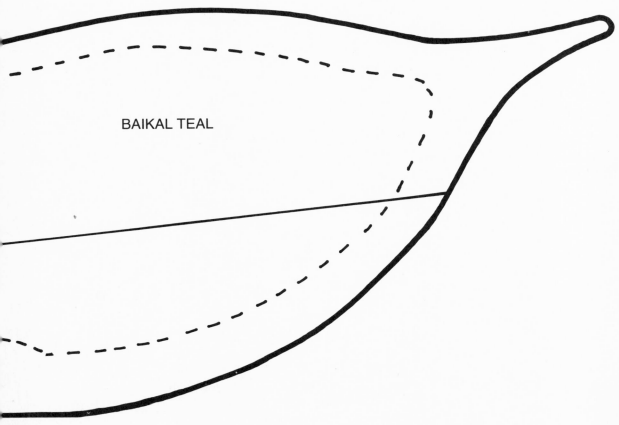

BAIKAL TEAL

BAIKAL TEAL

Plate 13 (*right*)   Remove staples to see and use full pattern.

DRAKE IN FLIGHT (UNDERSIDE)

A.H

STELLER'S EIDER: MALE

STELLER'S EIDER

POURED LEAD

STELLER'S EIDER

Plate 12 (*right*)   Remove staples to see and use full pattern.

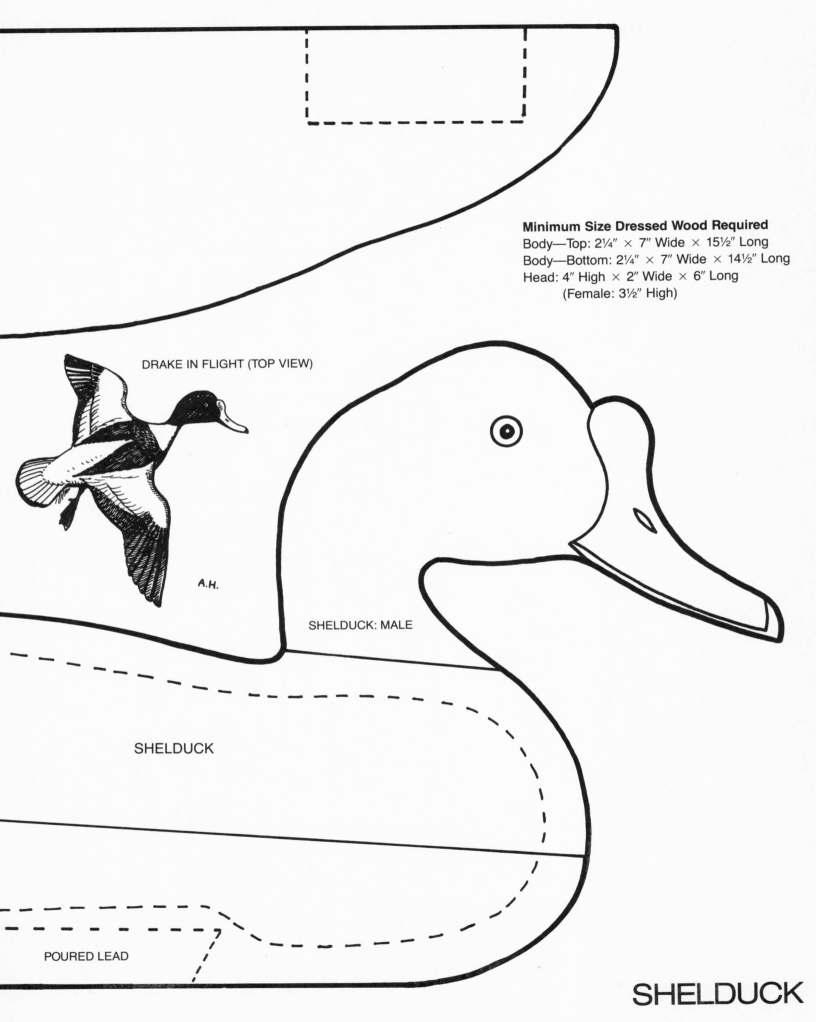

Minimum Size Dressed Wood Required
Body—Top: 2¼″ × 7″ Wide × 15½″ Long
Body—Bottom: 2¼″ × 7″ Wide × 14½″ Long
Head: 4″ High × 2″ Wide × 6″ Long
  (Female: 3½″ High)

DRAKE IN FLIGHT (TOP VIEW)

A.H.

SHELDUCK: MALE

SHELDUCK

POURED LEAD

SHELDUCK

Plate 11 (*right*)   Remove staples to see and use full pattern.

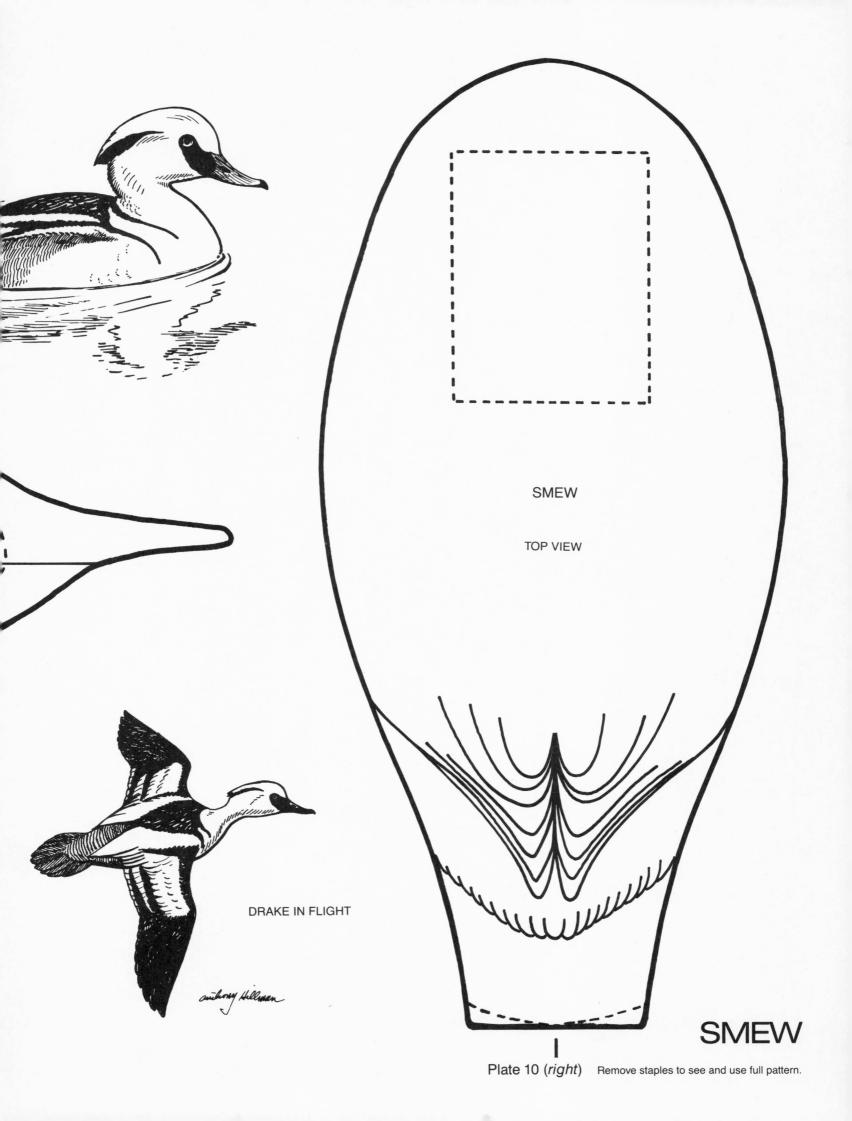

SMEW

TOP VIEW

DRAKE IN FLIGHT

anthony Hillman

SMEW

I

Plate 10 (*right*)   Remove staples to see and use full pattern.

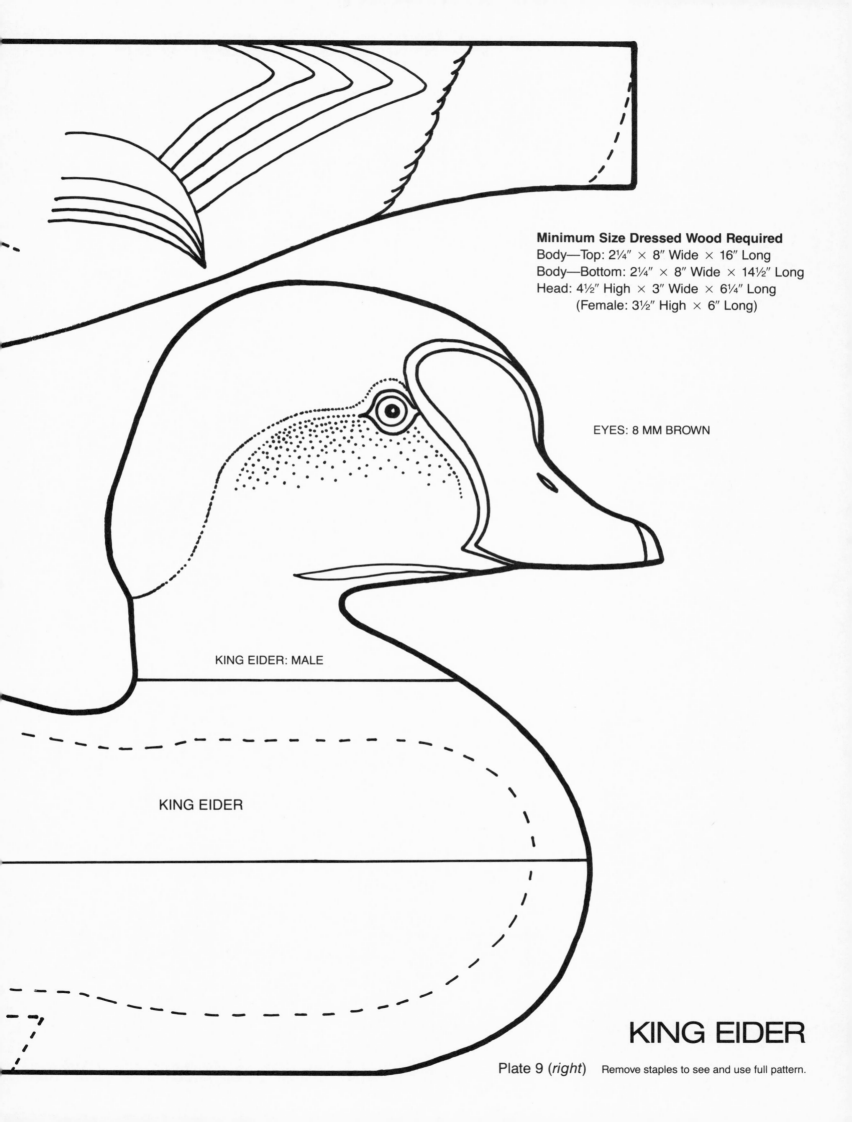

Minimum Size Dressed Wood Required
Body—Top: 2¼″ × 8″ Wide × 16″ Long
Body—Bottom: 2¼″ × 8″ Wide × 14½″ Long
Head: 4½″ High × 3″ Wide × 6¼″ Long
  (Female: 3½″ High × 6″ Long)

EYES: 8 MM BROWN

KING EIDER: MALE

KING EIDER

KING EIDER

Plate 9 (*right*)   Remove staples to see and use full pattern.

FULVOUS WHISTLING DUCK

TOP VIEW

The male and female of this species are similar in plumage.

FULVOUS WHISTLING DUCK

OURED LEAD

FULVOUS WHISTLING DUCK

Plate 8 (*right*)   Remove staples to see and use full pattern.

HARLEQUIN DUCK: MALE

HARLEQUIN DUCK

HARLEQUIN DUCK

Plate 7 (*right*)   Remove staples to see and use full pattern.

CINNAMON TEAL

TOP VIEW

CINNAMON TEAL: RELAXED

CINNAMON TEAL

CINNAMON TEAL

Plate 6 (*right*)   Remove staples to see and use full pattern.

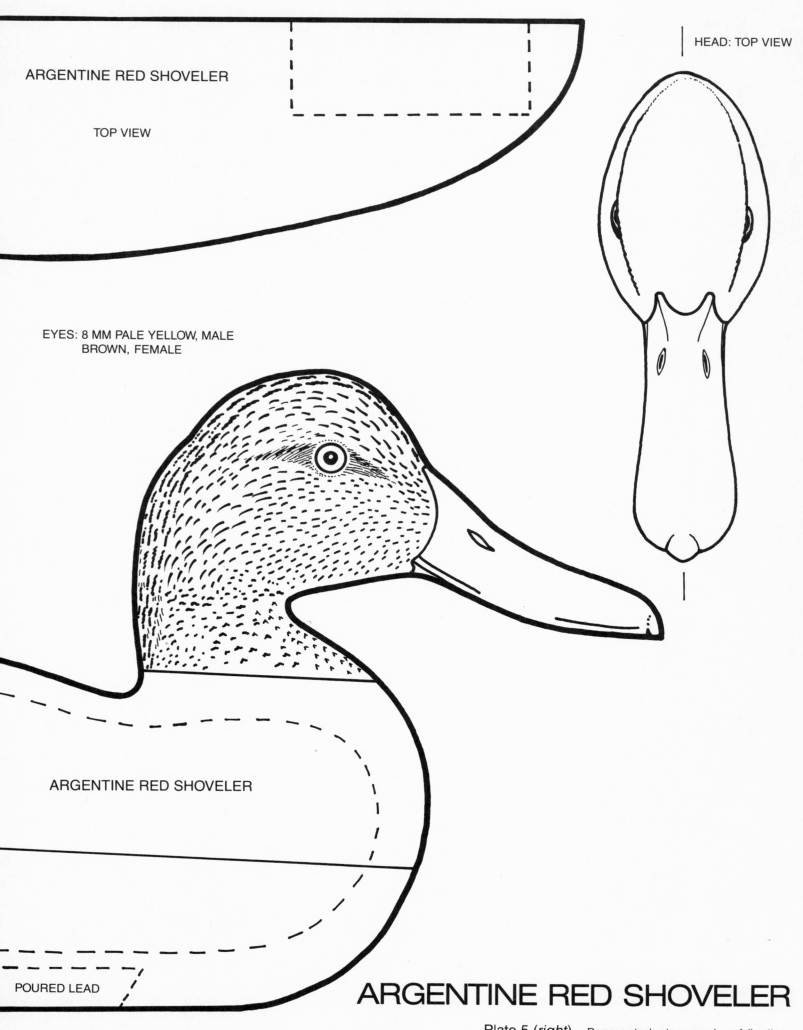

ARGENTINE RED SHOVELER

TOP VIEW

HEAD: TOP VIEW

EYES: 8 MM PALE YELLOW, MALE
BROWN, FEMALE

ARGENTINE RED SHOVELER

POURED LEAD

ARGENTINE RED SHOVELER

Plate 5 (*right*)   Remove staples to see and use full pattern.

WHITEFACED WHISTLING DUCK

TOP VIEW

Mutual preening is an activity
these waterfowl are noted for.

The male and female of this species are similar in plumage.

WHITEFACED WHISTLING DUCK

WHITEFACED WHISTLING DUCK

Plate 4 (*right*)   Remove staples to see and use full pattern.

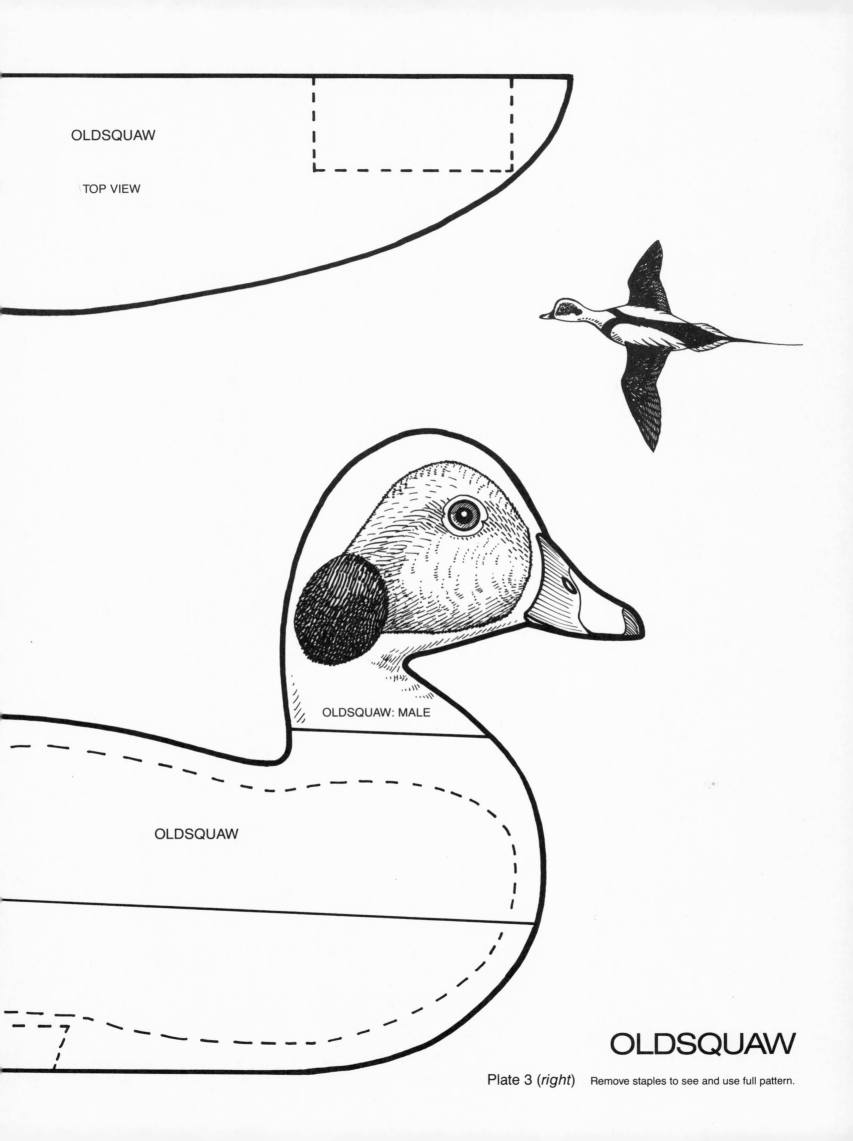

OLDSQUAW

TOP VIEW

OLDSQUAW: MALE

OLDSQUAW

OLDSQUAW

Plate 3 (*right*)   Remove staples to see and use full pattern.

RING-NECKED DUCK: MALE

RING-NECKED DUCK

RING-NECKED DUCK

Plate 2 (*right*)   Remove staples to see and use full pattern.

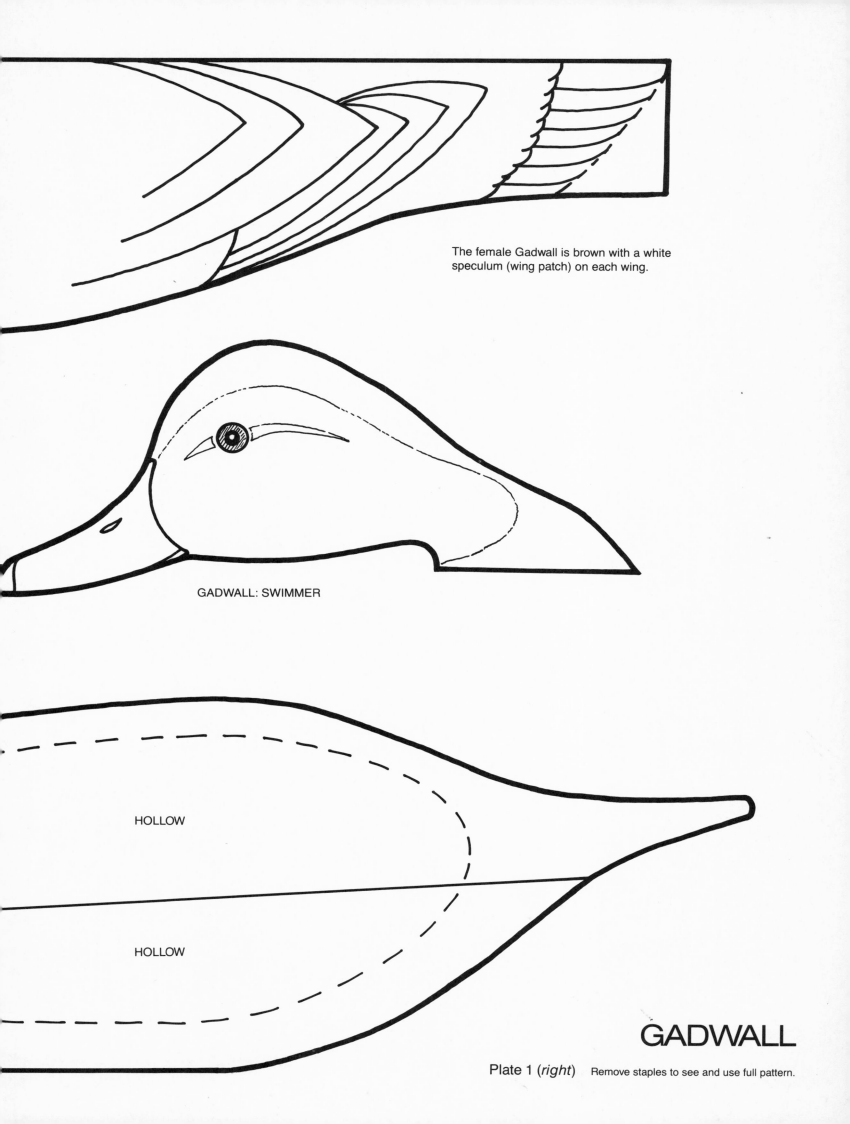

The female Gadwall is brown with a white
speculum (wing patch) on each wing.

GADWALL: SWIMMER

HOLLOW

HOLLOW

GADWALL

Plate 1 (*right*)   Remove staples to see and use full pattern.

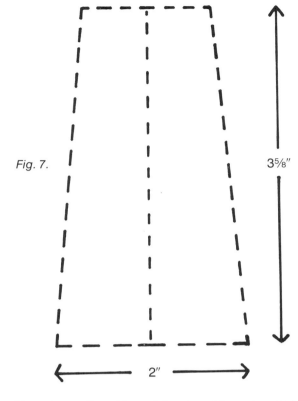

Fig. 7.

1³⁄₈″

3⁵⁄₈″

2″

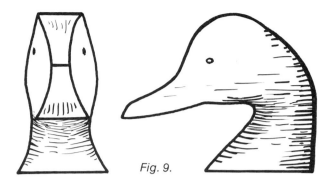

Fig. 9.

Carve off the corners of the neck and make it nice and round. Carve into the eye area and make a nice full cheek and round off the top of the head (Fig. 10). Put an 8D

Next, taper the sides of the head from top to bottom. Whittle this taper with a knife. Keep checking both sides (Fig. 7).

Look at the head from the top. Make sure that the cross-section line remains clearly marked. Using the profile pattern as a guide, mark a line across the upper side of the bill, perpendicular to the cross-section line, indicating where the top of the bill ends (Fig. 8). Mark another line across where the underside of the bill ends, corresponding to the line just made above, also perpendicular to the cross-section line. Generally, bill width can be determined by marking guidelines along the bill at a point halfway between the center line and the outside edge. Do this on each side of the cross-section line (Fig. 8).

Bill width can now be achieved by sawing or carving to these guidelines, making sure that both sides of the bill are symmetrical in relation to the cross-section line (Fig. 9). On the shoveler, you may want to leave the forward end of the bill as wide as the head and carve to correspond to the top view provided. Whether you carve the bill first or last is a matter of personal preference. You can mark the cuts for bill width and then start at the neck.

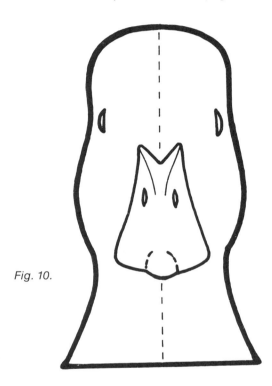

Fig. 10.

galvanized finishing nail through the neck and into the head to strengthen the neck. Fit the head to the body, using a block plane if necessary to get a nice fit. Glue and toenail the head in place, using 1″ brads (Fig. 11).

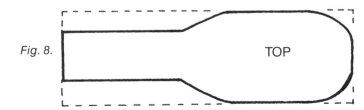

Fig. 8.

TOP

Fig. 11.

Completing the Carving

Sand the assembled decoy smooth and add the eyes. If you wish, you may paint the eyes on, and with a drop of varnish or clear nail polish on them they will really look good. Or you can use glass eyes. These are put in by drilling a hole the size of the eye (a 5/16″ bit for 8mm eyes), filling with plastic wood, and pushing in the eye. Wipe off plastic wood that squeezes out. With a little practice you can use the excess plastic wood to form the eyelids (Fig. 12).

If you want to float your decoy: using a straight chisel and a mallet, *carefully* cut a rectangular, beveled cavity in the bottom of the decoy (Figs. 13 and 14). Pouring in molten lead will assure a self-righting decoy.

There are a number of different devices available to melt lead. An old cast-iron pot, heated on a stove, with a small ladle for the lead, will probably be the easiest way for most people. Fishing-tackle supply houses also carry electric lead pots which are excellent.

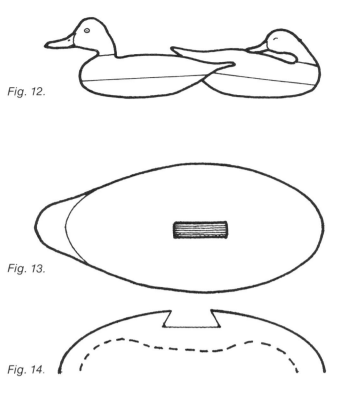

Fig. 12.

Fig. 13.

Fig. 14.

PAINTING OR FINISHING YOUR DECOY

There are as many different ways of painting a decoy as there are carvers of decoys. What we offer here are a few basic pointers. You may decide, while carving, to give the decoy a natural finish to bring out the beautiful grain present in the wood. Make sure all blemishes are sanded out, going over the wood again with 220 sandpaper for a really smooth finish. Stain your carving the color you desire. Allow to dry thoroughly. Apply a finish coat of varnish or shellac, following directions on the can.

To paint, the new wood should be primed with a good primer-sealer. Priming fills the pores of the wood and makes a suitable base to paint over. You can buy primer-sealer in any paint store. "Kilz," a primer-sealer made by Masterchem Industries, is an excellent product. Best of all, it can be covered with either oils or acrylics. After you prime-coat the carving, let it dry the required time, then sand with 220 sandpaper. This will take the roughness off, and give you a smooth base to paint over.

You can use oil or acrylic paints to finish your carving. The advantages of acrylics are that they dry quickly and that the brushes can be cleaned with soap and water. If using acrylics, apply a coat of acrylic primer on top of the oil-base primer to assure better adhesion during rough handling.

Besides the color plates in this book, good color references or live ducks are the best sources of colors and patterns. Among books with excellent color photographs of waterfowl are:

Ducks, Geese and Swans by Oscar J. Merne (St. Martin's Press, New York, 1974);

Waterfowl: Ducks, Geese and Swans of the World by Frank S. Todd (Harcourt Brace Jovanovich, New York, 1979); and

Wildfowl of the World by Eric Soothill and Peter James Whitehead (Blanford Press, Ltd., Poole, Dorset, England, 1978).

When using acrylics you can mix the colors in a plastic lid from a coffee can. When the paint has dried, you can bend the lid and peel the paint off. The lid can be used over and over again.

When painting decoys, the first step is to paint basic color areas. Flat, solid colors should be applied first. Detail can be added two ways. One is by stipple and dry-brush, effective methods of achieving soft shading and the illusion of vermiculations.

The other technique is the use of a brushed line, this being used in areas such as primary wing feathers and the sharp-edged markings found on most of the diving ducks. Where colors blend into each other with no discernible edge, wet-on-wet paint technique is in order.

An excellent book for detailed information on decoy-painting techniques is *Game Bird Carving* by Bruce Burk, published by Winchester Press. *Wild Fowl Decoys* by Joel Barber (Dover Publications, New York, 1954, 0-486-20011-6) offers many old-time painting tips, in addition to being the best introductory book available on the history of decoys. It also contains color plates of painted decoys.

With practice, you will develop your own painting style, which will further individualize your work. It can be as stylized or as detailed as you want it to be.